The Ultin Brownie Cookbook

The Best Brownie Recipes Known to Man

By

Heston Brown

HESTON **BROWN**

Thank you so much for buying my book! I want to give you a special gift!

Receive a special gift as a thank you for buying my book. Now you will be able to benefit from free and discounted book offers that are sent directly to your inbox every week.

To subscribe simply fill in the box below with your details and start reaping the rewards! A new deal will arrive every day and reminders will be sent so you never miss out. Fill in the box below to subscribe and get started!

https://heston-brown.getresponsepages.com

Subscribe
to our
newsletter

Your Email

Table of Contents

Recipe 1: Chocolate Caramel Brownie

Cooking Time: 45 minutes

Yield: 15

This is a sweet treat indeed: sweet enough to make a great Easter gift!

List of Ingredients:

- 1 cup butter
- 2 cups dark chocolate – chopped
- ¾ cup caster sugar
- 3 eggs – free-range – beaten
- 1 cup plain flour – sifted
- 2 packets caramel Easter eggs
- cocoa powder to dust

xxxxxxxxxxxxxxxxxxxxxxxxxxxxxxxxxxxxxxxxxxxxxxxx

Instructions:

Preheat the oven to 370°F.

Grease a rectangular slice pan and line it with baking paper.

In a saucepan, over a low flame, melt the butter and chocolate together.

Add the sugar, stirring until fully dissolved.

Remove from the heat and allow it to cool slightly.

Add the eggs and flour and combine well.

Pour into the prepared pan and press chocolate eggs into the top.

Place in the oven and bake for 25 minutes.

Allow it to cool before slicing it up.

Serve with a dusting of cocoa powder.

Recipe 2: Peanut Butter Brownie

Cooking Time: 50 minutes

Yield: 16

Yummy, chewy, peanut butter-flavoured brownies: is there a better brownie for the lunch box?

List of Ingredients:

- 1 cup butter – chopped
- 1 cup dark chocolate – chopped
- 3 eggs – free-range – beaten
- 1 ½ cups white sugar
- ¾ cup plain flour
- ¼ cup of cocoa powder
- 1 tsp. vanilla extract
- a pinch of salt
- ¾ cup smooth peanut butter

XXXXXXXXXXXXXXXXXXXXXXXXXXXXXXXXXXXXXXXXXXXXXXXXXX

Instructions:

Preheat the oven to 370°F.

Grease a square cake pan and line it with baking paper.

In a saucepan, over a low flame, melt the chocolate and butter together.

Remove from the heat.

Add the salt, vanilla, cocoa, flour, sugar, and eggs and combine well.

Pour into the prepared pan.

Spread peanut butter on top and, using a skewer, make swirl patterns.

Place in the oven and bake for 45 minutes.

Allow it to cool slightly and slice into desired size.

Delicious!

Recipe 3: Chocolate Brownies

Cooking Time: 45 minutes

Yield: 16

This is a classic brownie recipe that you will adore: moist, fresh brownies straight out of the oven.

List of Ingredients:

- 1 ¼ cups of butter
- 2 cups of dark chocolate – chopped
- 1 cup brown sugar
- 3 eggs – free-range – beaten
- 1 tsp. vanilla extract
- ¾ cup of plain flour
- 2 Tbsp. cocoa powder
- ¼ cup pecans – chopped

xxxxxxxxxxxxxxxxxxxxxxxxxxxxxxxxxxxxxxxxxxxxxxxx

Instructions:

Preheat the oven to 370°F.

Grease a square cake tin and line it with baking paper.

In a saucepan, over a low flame, melt the butter, sugar, and chocolate together.

Stir this constantly before pouring it into a bowl to cool.

Add the eggs and vanilla and mix well.

Sift the cocoa and flour into the chocolate mixture and combine well.

Pour the mixture into the prepared pan and top with pecans.

Place in the oven for 25 minutes, or until the brownie is cooked and firm to the touch.

Set aside to cool and then slice into desired portions. Enjoy.

Recipe 4: Spiced Orange and Raisin Brownies

Cooking Time: 1 hour

Yleld: 12

Spice things up with this delicious, orange-flavored fruit and nut brownie recipe.

List of Ingredients:

- 1 ½ cups butter – chopped
- 1 cup chocolate – chopped
- 1 ½ cups caster sugar
- 3 eggs – free-range
- 2 tsp. orange zest
- 1 ½ tsp. vanilla essence
- ¾ cup plain flour
- ¼ cup cocoa powder
- 1 tsp. mixed spice – ground
- 1 cup raisins
- 1/3 cup mixed peel

XXXXXXXXXXXXXXXXXXXXXXXXXXXXXXXXXXXXXXXXXXXXXXXX

Instructions:

Preheat the oven to 380°F.

Grease a baking pan and line it with baking paper.

In a saucepan, over a low flame, melt the butter and chocolate together.

Remove from the heat and allow it to cool slightly.

In a bowl add the eggs and sugar.

Using electric beaters, beat them together until pale.

Add the chocolate mixture, zest, and vanilla.

Add sifted flour, cocoa, and mixed spice, folding until smooth.

Add the fruits and peels and mix through.

Pour into the prepared pan and place in the oven to bake for 40 minutes.

Serve warm.

Recipe 5: Raspberry Brownie

Cooking Time: 45 minutes

Yield: 12

The combination of good-quality dark chocolate and the sweetness of summer raspberries is a winning one.

List of Ingredients:

- 1 ¼ cup butter – chopped

- 2 cups dark chocolate – chopped

- 3 eggs – free-range – beaten

- 2 cups brown sugar

- ¾ cup plain flour

- 2/3 cup cocoa powder

- 2 cups fresh raspberries

XXXXXXXXXXXXXXXXXXXXXXXXXXXXXXXXXXXXXXXXXXXXXXXXXX

Instructions:

Preheat the oven to 350°F.

Grease a slice pan and line it with baking paper.

In a saucepan, over a medium flame, melt the butter and chocolate, stirring continuously.

Allow it to cool.

In a bowl, combine the sugar and eggs until combined.

Sift the cocoa and flour into the egg mixture and gently mix together.

Slowly add the chocolate mixture and fold together.

Pour into the prepared pan and place raspberries on the top layer of the brownie.

Place in the oven to bake for about 40 minutes.

Allow the brownies to cool before slicing it up.

Delicious!

Recipe 6: Pumpkin Cheesecake Brownies

Cooking Time: 2 hours

Yield: 24

Never had pumpkin and chocolate together? Try it! It's simply delicious!

List of Ingredients:

- 1 ¼ cups butter – chopped
- 2 ½ cups dark chocolate – chopped
- 1 cup of caster sugar
- 3 eggs – free-range
- 1 ¼ cups plain flour
- ¼ cup cocoa powder
- ¼ cup sour cream
- 1 packet cream cheese – softened
- 1 cup pumpkin puree

xxxxxxxxxxxxxxxxxxxxxxxxxxxxxxxxxxxxxxxxxxxxxxxxxx

Instructions:

Preheat the oven to 350°F.

Grease a square cake pan and line it with a baking paper.

In a saucepan, over a low flame, melt together the chocolate and butter.

Remove from the heat and add 2/3 cup of the sugar and 2 eggs, combining well.

Add the cocoa, flour, and sour cream and mix together well.

Using electric beaters, beat the sugar and cheese together until creamy.

Add the egg and pumpkin and beat until combined.

Alternately, spoon a dollop of each mixture into the prepared pan.

Use a skewer to make a marbled effect on the surface.

Place in the oven and bake for 40 minutes.

Allow it to cool before slicing it up.

Recipe 7: Pistachio Brownies

Cooking Time: 55 minutes

Yield: 8

A nutty-flavoured, freshly cooked brownie is an afternoon tea delight!

List of Ingredients:

- ½ cup of butter
- 1 cup dark chocolate – chopped
- ½ cup brown sugar
- 1 tsp. vanilla essence
- 1 egg – free-range
- 1 egg yolk – free-range
- 1/3 cup plain flour
- ¼ cup pistachio chopped

xxxxxxxxxxxxxxxxxxxxxxxxxxxxxxxxxxxxxxxxxxxxxxxx

Instructions:

Preheat the oven to 350°F and grease a loaf pan and then line it with baking paper.

In a saucepan, over a low flame, melt the chocolate and butter, stirring as you go.

Allow it to cool.

Add the sugar and vanilla to the chocolate mixture and whisk together.

Add the eggs and whisk together until smooth.

Add the pistachios and combine.

Pour into the prepared pan and bake for 35 minutes.

Allow it to cool and slice it up – I like to serve it a little warm.

So yum!

Recipe 8: One-Bowl Brownies

Cooking Time: 50 minutes

Yield: 16

Whip up this deliciously easy brownie recipe for everyone to enjoy - even your dishwasher!

List of Ingredients:

- 1 cup butter
- 2 cups dark chocolate – chopped
- ¾ cup brown sugar
- 1 tsp. vanilla essence
- 1 cup plain flour
- 3 eggs – free-range – beaten
- ½ cup dark choc bits
- ½ cup pecans – chopped

XXXXXXXXXXXXXXXXXXXXXXXXXXXXXXXXXXXXXXXXXXXXXXXX

Instructions:

Preheat the oven to 370°F.

Grease a square cake pan and line it with baking paper.

In a saucepan, over a low flame, melt the butter and chocolate together.

Add the brown sugar, stirring until fully dissolved.

Add the eggs and flour, stirring well to combine.

Add the chocolate bits and nuts, stirring well.

Pour into the prepared pan and place in the oven to bake for 40 minutes.

Allow it to cool before slicing it up.

Recipe 9: Gingerbread Brownies

Cooking Time: 40 minutes

Yield: 9

Gingerbread brownies are wonderfully festive brownies that make delicious Christmas gifts.

List of Ingredients:

- 2 cups butter – chopped
- 2 ½ cups dark chocolate – chopped
- 4 eggs – free-range
- 1 1/3 cups brown sugar
- 1 1/3 cups plain flour
- ½ tsp. baking powder
- ½ tsp. cinnamon – ground
- ½ tsp. ginger – ground
- ½ tsp. nutmeg – ground
- 1/3 cup cocoa – sifted
- icing sugar to dust

xxxxxxxxxxxxxxxxxxxxxxxxxxxxxxxxxxxxxxxxxxxxxxxx

Instructions:

Preheat the oven to 360°F.

Grease a cake tin and line it with baking paper.

In a saucepan, over a low flame, melt the chocolate and butter together, stirring until smooth.

Allow it to cool slightly.

Beat 1 egg at a time into the chocolate mixture.

Add the spices, baking powder, sugar, and flour and combine well.

Fold in the cocoa.

Pour into the prepared pan and bake for 25 minutes.

Set aside to cool before slicing into squares.

Dust with icing sugar and serve them up fresh!

Recipe 10: Choc Cherry Brownies

Cooking Time: 55 minutes

Yield: 16

Low in calories and huge in flavor – this recipe has a festive

feel about it.

List of Ingredients:

- 1/3 cup almond meal
- 1/3 cup desiccated coconut
- 1/3 cup cocoa powder
- ¼ cup arrowroot
- ¼ cup brown rice flour
- 2 ½ tsp. xylitol
- 1 tsp. cinnamon – ground
- ½ cup maple syrup
- 2 eggs – free-range
- 1/3 cup coconut oil – melted
- 1/3 cup Greek-style yogurt
- 1 ¼ cups cherries – pitted and halved
- 1 tsp. brandy
- 1 cup dark chocolate – melted and cooled
- 2 tsp. coconut – flaked
- a pinch of sea salt

xxxxxxxxxxxxxxxxxxxxxxxxxxxxxxxxxxxxxxxxxxxxxxxxxxx

Instructions:

Preheat the oven to 360°F.

Grease a square cake pan and line it with baking paper.

In a large bowl, add the almond meal, coconut, cocoa, arrowroot, flour, xylitol, salt, and cinnamon and combined well.

Make a well in the middle of the mixture.

In a jug, whisk the eggs, oil, syrup, and yogurt together until smooth.

In a microwave combine the brandy cherries and syrup and heat on high for 90 seconds.

Add the cherry syrup to the egg mixture.

Add the wet Ingredients to the dry Ingredients and mix well.

Pour into the prepared pan.

Scatter the coconut over the top.

Place in the oven and bake for 30 minutes.

Allow it to cool before slicing it up.

Recipe 11: Cheesecake Brownies

Cooking Time: 1 hour and 10 minutes

Yield: 18

Yummy, creamy slices of heavenly goodness – this moist brownie recipe will have you sneaking another piece.

List of Ingredients:

- 1 ¼ cups dark chocolate – chopped
- ¾ cup of butter
- 3 eggs – free-range
- ½ cup plain flour
- 1 cup caster sugar
- 2 Tbsp. cocoa powder – sifted
- 1 packet of cream cheese
- ¼ cup sour cream

XXXXXXXXXXXXXXXXXXXXXXXXXXXXXXXXXXXXXXXXXXXXXXXXXX

Instructions:

Preheat oven to 350°F.

Grease a baking pan and line it with a baking paper.

In a saucepan, over a low flame, melt the chocolate and butter together and stir until smooth.

Allow it to cool.

Add 2 eggs and whisk until combined.

In a bowl, add the flour, ½ cup caster sugar, and cocoa.

Pour in the chocolate mixture and combine well.

In a bowl, use electric beaters to beat the sour cream, cream cheese and the remaining sugar together.

Add the remaining egg and combine well.

Alternately, spoon a dollop of each mixture into the prepared pan.

Grab a skewer and create a swirl pattern.

Place in the oven and bake for 50 minutes.

Allow it to cool and slice it up.

Enjoy!

Recipe 12: Rocky Road Brownie

Cooking Time: 40 minutes

Yield: 18

So delicious and rich in chocolatey flavor, that's what

makes this a great dessert!

List of Ingredients:

- 2 ½ cups dark chocolate – chopped

- 1 ¼ cups butter – chopped

- ¾ cup caster sugar

- 3 eggs – free-range – beaten

- 1 ¼ cups plain flour

- ½ cup of pink and white marshmallows – cut in half

- ½ cup of whole peanuts – roasted and chopped

XXXXXXXXXXXXXXXXXXXXXXXXXXXXXXXXXXXXXXXXXXXXXXXX

Instructions:

Preheat the oven to 370°F.

Then grease a loaf pan and line it with a baking paper.

In a saucepan, over a low flame, melt the butter and chocolate together.

Add the sugar, stirring until it fully dissolves.

Remove from the heat and allow it to cool slightly.

Add the egg and flour, stirring well.

Add the marshmallows and peanuts, folding them in well.

Pour into the prepared pan and place in the oven to bake for 20 minutes.

Allow it to set before slicing it up!

Recipe 13: Butterscotch Brownies

Cooking Time: 45 minutes

Yield: 16

Mix things up with this butterscotch brownie recipe. It's

nutty caramel flavors will tempt all hungry bellies.

List of Ingredients:

- ¾ cup butter – chopped
- 1 cup brown sugar
- 2 eggs – free-range – beaten
- 1 tsp. vanilla extract
- 1 cup plain flour – sifted
- 2 tsp. baking powder
- ½ cup roasted peanuts – chopped
- 1 cup Jersey caramels – chopped
- icing sugar to dust

xxxxxxxxxxxxxxxxxxxxxxxxxxxxxxxxxxxxxxxxxxxxxx

Instructions:

Preheat the oven to 370°F.

Grease a square cake pan and line it with baking paper.

In a saucepan, over a medium flame, melt the butter.

Add the butter to a bowl along with the vanilla, sugar, and eggs and combine well.

Fold in the flour, peanuts, and baking powder.

Pour into the prepared pan and top with the caramels.

Place in the oven and bake for 25 minutes, or until the top is crispy.

Allow it to cool and slice it into squares.

Yum!

Recipe 14: Choc Peppermint Brownie

Cooking Time: 1 hour

Yield: 16

Minty fresh brownies are irresistible and oh so moreish –
these are a must-try recipe.

List of Ingredients:

- 1 ¼ cup butter – chopped

- 1 cup dark, mint chocolate – chopped

- 3 eggs – free-range – beaten

- 2/3 cup plain flour – sifted

- ¼ cup cocoa powder – sifted

- ¾ cup icing sugar

- 1 tsp. milk

- ¼ tsp peppermint essence

- 1 Peppermint Crisp chocolate bar – chopped

xxxxxxxxxxxxxxxxxxxxxxxxxxxxxxxxxxxxxxxxxxxxxxxx

Instructions:

Preheat the oven to 380°F.

Grease a square cake pan and line it with baking paper.

In a saucepan, over a low flame, melt together the butter and the chocolate.

Remove from the heat and then add the sugar, stirring until incorporated.

Allow it to cool slightly.

Add the egg, flour, and cocoa, mixing until well combined.

Pour into the prepared pan and place in the oven to bake for 25 minutes.

Allow it to cool completely.

Meanwhile, in a bowl, add the milk, Peppermint essence. and icing sugar together, mixing until smooth.

Pour the icing over the brownie and scatter the crushed Peppermint Crisp on top.

Allow it to set before slicing it up.

Ready for eating!

Recipe 15: Deluxe Brownies

Cooking Time: 1 hour and 10 minutes

Yield: 16

All of your favourite Ingredients rolled into one delightful brownie recipe.

List of Ingredients:

- 1 cup butter – chopped
- 1 cup dark chocolate – chopped
- 1 cup of white chocolate - chopped
- 3 eggs – free-range – beaten
- 1 ½ cups white sugar
- 1 cup plain flour
- ¼ cup cocoa powder
- 1 tsp. vanilla extract
- 1 cup macadamia nuts – chopped
- 1 cup fresh raspberries
- a pinch of salt

XXXXXXXXXXXXXXXXXXXXXXXXXXXXXXXXXXXXXXXXXXXXXXX

Instructions:

Preheat the oven to 370°F.

Grease a square cake tin and line it with baking paper.

In a saucepan, over a low flame, melt the butter and dark chocolate together.

Remove from the heat and add the eggs, stirring as you do until well combined.

Add the sugar, flour, cocoa, vanilla, white chocolate, macadamias, salt, and raspberries and combine well.

Pour in the prepared pan and place in the oven for 45 minutes.

Allow it to cool and slice up into squares.

Delicious!

Recipe 16: Fudgy Avocado Brownies

Cooking Time: 50 minutes

Yield: 16

Gluten- and dairy-free, this brownie treat is definitely a healthy one!

List of Ingredients:

- 1 ½ cups dark chocolate – chopped
- 2 avocados – chopped
- 3 eggs – free-range
- ¼ cup cacao powder
- ½ cup almond meal
- 1 ½ cups coconut sugar
- 1 ½ cups walnuts – chopped
- a pinch of salt

XXXXXXXXXXXXXXXXXXXXXXXXXXXXXXXXXXXXXXXXXXXXXXXXXX

Instructions:

Preheat the oven to 370°F.

Grease a square cake tin and line it with baking paper.

In a saucepan, over a low flame, melt the chocolate.

In a food processor, blitz the avocado, eggs, cacao, and salt together until smooth.

Place in a bowl and add the almond meal, folding well.

Add the chocolate mixture and combine well.

Pour into the prepared pan and place in the oven to bake for 30 minutes.

Allow it to cool before slicing it up!

Recipe 17: Chocolate Cranberry Brownie

Cooking Time: 1 hour

Yield: 6

Antioxidants and the luscious taste of chocolate makes this brownie a healthy, sweet treat.

List of Ingredients:

- 1 ¼ cups butter – cubed
- 2 cups dark chocolate – chopped
- 1 ¼ cups plain flour
- 1/3 cup cocoa
- ½ tsp. baking powder
- 4 eggs – free-range – beaten
- ½ cup dried cranberries
- ¾ cup of brown sugar

xxxxxxxxxxxxxxxxxxxxxxxxxxxxxxxxxxxxxxxxxxxxxxxxx

Instructions:

Preheat the oven to 360°F.

Grease a square cake pan and line it with baking paper.

In a saucepan, over a low flame, melt the butter and chocolate together and stir until smooth.

Remove from the heat and allow it to cool.

In a large bowl, sift the cocoa and flour together.

Add the chocolate mixture, eggs, sugar, and cranberries and mix well.

Pour into the prepared pan and place in the oven to bake for 35 minutes.

Allow it to cool for 10 minutes and slice up,

Serve it up warm!

Recipe 18: Zucchini and Cacao Brownie

Cooking Time: 35 minutes

Yield: 20

A healthy brownie that stays moist and delicious – great for lunch boxes and growing kids!

List of Ingredients:

- 1 ¼ cups brown sugar
- ½ cup olive oil
- 2 eggs – free-range
- 2 cups zucchini – grated, with excess water removed
- 2 cups self- raising flour
- ½ cup raw cacao
- 2/3 cup walnuts – chopped
- 1 cup no-added-sugar chocolate – chopped
- a pinch of salt

xxxxxxxxxxxxxxxxxxxxxxxxxxxxxxxxxxxxxxxxxxxxxxxxx

Instructions:

Preheat the oven to 370°F.

Grease a baking pan and line it with baking paper.

In a bowl, whisk the eggs, oil, and vanilla together.

Add the zucchini, flour, cacao, salt, and walnuts and mix well.

Pour into the prepared pan and place in the oven to bake for 20 minutes.

Allow it to cool before slicing it up!

Recipe 19: Rum and Raisin Brownies

Cooking Time: 1 hour and 10 minutes

Yield: 25

This is a grown-up brownie recipe – why should the kids have all the fun?

List of Ingredients:

- 1 cup Chilean Flame raisins
- ½ cup dark rum
- 1 cup butter – chopped
- 2 ½ cups dark chocolate – chopped
- ¾ cup brown sugar
- 2 eggs – free-range – beaten
- 1 ½ cups plain flour
- 1 cup walnuts – chopped
- ¼ cup sour cream

xxxxxxxxxxxxxxxxxxxxxxxxxxxxxxxxxxxxxxxxxxxxxxx

Instructions:

In a saucepan, over a low flame, combine the raisins and rum and cook for 2 minutes.

Remove from the heat and allow them to soak, covered, for 4 hours.

Preheat the oven to 370°F.

Grease a square cake pan and line it with baking paper.

In a saucepan, over a low flame, melt the butter and chocolate together until smooth.

Remove from the heat and allow it to cool slightly.

Add the eggs, sugar, and flour, sour cream, walnuts, and the raisin mixture and mix it together well.

Pour into the prepared pan and place in the oven to bake for 45 minutes.

Set aside to cool before slicing into desired size.

Eat it up! These go great with a hot cup of cocoa.

Recipe 20: Triple Choc Brownies

Cooking Time: 50 minutes

Yield: 8

Very decadent and rich in flavor, these brownies are guaranteed to please any chocolate connoisseur.

List of Ingredients:

- 1 ½ cups dark chocolate – chopped
- 1 ½ cups butter – chopped
- 3 eggs – free-range – beaten
- 1 tsp. vanilla extract
- 1 ½ cups milk chocolate – chopped
- 2 ¼ cups walnuts – chopped
- 1/3 cup plain flour
- ¼ cup cocoa powder
- vanilla ice-cream and hot fudge sauce to serve

xxxxxxxxxxxxxxxxxxxxxxxxxxxxxxxxxxxxxxxxxxxxxxx

Instructions:

Preheat the oven to 370°F.

Grease a baking pan and line it with baking paper.

In a saucepan, over a low flame, melt the butter and chocolate together until melted.

Remove from the heat and allow it to cool slightly.

Add the sugar, eggs, vanilla, and finally the walnuts to the chocolate mixture.

Add sifted cocoa and flour and fold together well.

Pour into the prepared pan and place in the oven to bake for 30 minutes.

Set aside to cool before slicing into desired portions.

Serve warm with ice-cream and hot fudge sauce.

Recipe 21: Chocolate Coconut Brownie

Cooking Time: 1 hour

Yield: 12

You cannot beat the marriage of coconut and chocolate – a match made in heaven.

List of Ingredients:

- 1 ½ cups butter – chopped

- 1 ½ cups dark chocolate – chopped

- 3 eggs – free-range – beaten

- 1 ½ cups caster sugar

- ½ cup desiccated coconut

- 1 tsp. vanilla essence

- 1 cup plain flour – sifted

- 1/3 cup cocoa – sifted

- icing sugar to dust

xxxxxxxxxxxxxxxxxxxxxxxxxxxxxxxxxxxxxxxxxxxxxxx

Instructions:

Preheat the oven to 360°F.

Grease a loaf pan and line it with baking paper.

In a saucepan, over a low flame, melt the butter and chocolate together until melted.

Remove from the heat to cool slightly.

In a large bowl, combine the vanilla, coconut, eggs, and sugar together.

In a separate bowl, mix the cocoa and flour together.

Add the chocolate mixture to the egg mixture and stir together well.

Add the flour mixture and fold together gently.

Pour into the prepared pan and place in the oven to bake for 35 minutes or until firm.

Allow it to cool before dusting with icing sugar.

Recipe 22: Rich Beetroot and Choc Brownies

Cooking Time: 50 minutes

Yield: 20

The earthy goodness of beetroot keeps this brownie deliciously moist.

List of Ingredients:

- 1 ¾ cups beetroot – chopped
- 1 ¼ cups butter – chopped
- 1 ¼ cups brown sugar
- 2 cups dark chocolate – chopped
- 3 eggs – free-range – beaten
- ½ cup plain flour
- 1/3 cup cocoa powder
- ¼ tsp. nutmeg – ground
- ¼ tsp. cinnamon – ground
- 1 cup walnuts – chopped
- icing sugar to dust

xxxxxxxxxxxxxxxxxxxxxxxxxxxxxxxxxxxxxxxxxxxxxxxxxx

Instructions:

Preheat the oven to 370°F.

Grease a square cake pan and line it with a baking paper.

Using a food processor, finely chop the beetroot.

In a saucepan, over a medium flame, add the beetroot, flour, cocoa, cinnamon, and nutmeg and combine well.

Add sifted flour and walnuts, folding them into the mixture.

Pour into the prepared pan and place in the oven to bake for 30 minutes until firm.

Dust with icing sugar and slice up.

Recipe 23: Macadamia and White Chocolate Brownie

Cooking Time: 50 minutes

Yield: 16

Creamy white chocolate and creamy macadamias make this a creamy delight!

List of Ingredients:

- 1 ¾ cups white chocolate – chopped
- 1 ½ cups butter – cubed
- 1 cup caster sugar
- 3 eggs – free-range – beaten
- 1 tsp. vanilla extract
- 1 cup macadamia nuts – chopped
- ¾ cup plain flour

XXXXXXXXXXXXXXXXXXXXXXXXXXXXXXXXXXXXXXXXXXXXX

Instructions:

Preheat the oven to 360°F.

Grease a square cake pan and line it with baking paper.

In a saucepan, over a low flame, melt the butter and chocolate together until melted.

Remove from the heat and allow it to cool slightly.

Add the eggs, sugar, and vanilla and mix well.

Fold in the flour and nuts until combined.

Pour into the prepared pan and place in the oven to bake for 35 minutes.

Serve it up warm.

Recipe 24: Lemon and Coconut Brownies

Cooking Time: 50 minutes

Yield: 15

Tantalize your taste buds by adding a little citrus twist on the traditional brownie.

List of Ingredients:

- 1 ½ cups butter
- 2 cups caster sugar
- 1 ½ cups plain flour
- 4 eggs – free-range
- 3 tsp. lemon zest
- 1 cup desiccated coconut
- Icing sugar to dust
- ¼ cup fresh lemon juice

xxxxxxxxxxxxxxxxxxxxxxxxxxxxxxxxxxxxxxxxxxxxxxxxx

Instructions:

Preheat the oven to 370°F.

Grease a baking pan and line it with baking paper.

In a saucepan, over a medium flame, melt the butter.

Then remove the pan from the heat. Add the sugar, stirring until incorporated.

Add an egg at a time, whisking constantly.

Add sifted flour, the coconut, zest, and juice and fold together well.

Pour into the prepared pan and place in the oven to bake for 35 minutes.

Allow it to cool before dusting with icing sugar and slicing into squares.

Zesty!

Recipe 25: Sugar-Free Brownie

Cooking Time: 35 minutes

Yield: 16

Guilt-free brownies? Perfect! Indulge in these delicious sweet treats knowing there is no sugar in this recipe.

List of Ingredients:

- 1 can of black beans
- 12 fresh dates – pitted
- ¼ cup coconut oil
- ¼ cup milk
- 1 tsp. vanilla bean paste
- ½ cup raw cacao
- 1 tsp. walnuts – halved
- 1 tsp. pistachios
- 1 tsp. hazelnuts – halved

xxxxxxxxxxxxxxxxxxxxxxxxxxxxxxxxxxxxxxxxxxxxxxx

Instructions:

Preheat the oven to 370°F.

Grease a square cake pan and line it with baking paper.

In a food processor, blitz the beans, dates, oil, vanilla, and milk together until smooth.

Add cacao and combine well.

Pour into the prepared pan and arrange the nuts on top.

Place in the oven and bake for 20 minutes.

Allow it to cool and slice up!

About the Author

Heston Brown is an accomplished chef and successful e-book author from Palo Alto California. After studying cooking at The New England Culinary Institute, Heston stopped briefly in Chicago where he was offered head chef at some of the city's most prestigious restaurants. Brown decide that he missed the rolling hills and sunny weather of California and moved back to his home state to open up his own catering company and give private cooking classes.

Heston lives in California with his beautiful wife of 18 years and his two daughters who also have aspirations to follow in their father's footsteps and pursue careers in the culinary arts. Brown is well known for his delicious fish and chicken dishes and teaches these recipes as well as many others to his students.

When Heston gave up his successful chef position in Chicago and moved back to California, a friend suggested he use the internet to share his recipes with the world and so he did! To date, Heston Brown has written over 1000 e-books that contain recipes, cooking tips, business strategies for catering companies and a self-help book he wrote from personal experience.

He claims his wife has been his inspiration throughout many of his endeavours and continues to be his partner in business as well as life. His greatest joy is having all three women in his life in the kitchen with him cooking their favourite meal while his favourite jazz music plays in the background.

Author's Afterthoughts

Thank you !!!

Thank you to all the readers who invested time and money into my book! I cherish every one of you and hope you took the same pleasure in reading it as I did in writing it.

Out of all of the books out there, you chose mine and for that I am truly grateful. It makes the effort worth it when I know my readers are enjoying my work from beginning to end.

Please take a few minutes to write an Amazon review so that others can benefit from your opinions and insight. Your review will help countless other readers make an informed choice

Thank you so much,

Heston Brown

Printed in Great Britain
by Amazon

18770193R00051